Red Riding Hood and the Tassie Tiger

By Dawn McMillan

Illustrated by Melanie Matthews

Pearson Australia
(a division of Pearson Australia Group Pty Ltd)
707 Collins Street, Melbourne, Victoria 3008
PO Box 23360, Melbourne, Victoria 8012
www.pearson.com.au

First published 2014 by Pearson Australia
2021 2020 2019 2018
10 9 8 7 6 5 4 3 2 1

Publisher: Sabine Bolick
Project Managers: Tamara Pirois and Rachel Davis
Lead Editor: Kerry Nagle
Editor: Anne McKenna
Cover and series designer: Jenny Grigg
Designers: Jennifer Johnston and Nina Heryanto
Copyright & Pictures Editor: Julia Weaver
Mac Operator: Rob Curulli
Cover art: Melanie Matthews
Illustrator: Melanie Matthews
Printed in Australia by the SOS Print + Media Group

ISBN 978 1 4860 0748 6

Pearson Australia Group Pty Ltd ABN 40 004 245 943

Disclaimer
Some of the images used in *Red Riding Hood and the Tassie Tiger* might have associations with deceased Indigenous Australians. Please be aware that these images might cause sadness or distress in Aboriginal or Torres Strait Islander communities.

Contents

Characters

- Narrator
- Dad
- Red Riding Hood
- Thylacine
- Police Officer Lee
- Elderly Man
- Shop Owner
- Teenagers 1, 2 and 3
- Gran

Props

- scooter and helmet
- vegetables – real or cardboard vegetables
- spade
- large gumboots
- backpack
- cardboard police car
- shop sign
- cardboard sports car
- Gran's house – painted cardboard

Act 1

Too small for her boots

Scene

The vegetable garden at Red Riding Hood's and Dad's home. RED RIDING HOOD is wearing Dad's gumboots. DAD is holding a spade.

Narrator (*facing audience*) I'm sure you know the fairytale about Red Riding Hood. Well, here's a new Red Riding Hood story. Our Red Riding Hood lives with her dad in a house in the suburbs. They like to work in their vegetable garden.

Dad Just look at you, Red Riding Hood. What on earth are you doing in my gumboots?

Red Riding Hood I can't find mine, so I'm using yours.

Dad Watch out for our lettuce seedlings! You're stomping around like a giant. Hey, look at these carrots. I think we grow the best carrots in Australia. Pull one out and see how far down it goes.

Red Riding Hood (*pulling the carrot and laughing*) All the way to New Zealand!

Dad Gosh, one carrot will last us for a couple of meals. We'll never eat them all.

Red Riding Hood And the silverbeet, Dad. They're like trees! And the beans are the size of sausages!

Dad Yes, everything's gone crazy this year. Must be all that chook poo and the rain.

We've got enough vegetables to feed the neighbourhood – and Gran. She loves our vegies.

Red Riding Hood She sure does. And she doesn't have time to grow her own. Carrots. Silverbeet. I'll take her some tomatoes too, and some beans.

Dad Good idea. Get your scooter from the shed and your backpack. We'll load you up and you'll be set to go.

Red Riding Hood goes offstage and returns with her scooter, helmet and backpack. She and Dad pack vegetables into the backpack.

Red Riding Hood I'm ready, Dad. Gran will love all this healthy, fresh, yummy food.

Dad (*leaning on the spade and laughing*) Right. But before you go, you might like to find something more suitable to wear on your feet!

Act 2

An interesting character

Scene

The main street. Red Riding Hood is riding her scooter and wearing her backpack, helmet and boots that fit. Thylacine approaches.

Narrator Red Riding Hood sets out on her scooter, along the footpath. She hums her favourite song. On the way to Gran's, she meets a very interesting character.

Thylacine (*craftily*) Why, hello there. It's Red Riding Hood, I believe. Nice to meet you, at last. Do you know who I am?

Red Riding Hood Yes, of course. I recognise your sandy-coloured coat and your chocolate-brown stripes. And your stiff tail, too. You're a thylacine. That's your proper name.

Thylacine Is that so? You're very clever. Not too many people know a thylacine when they see one.

Red Riding Hood So, Thylacine, how do you know my name? And what are you doing here? Aren't you scared of the traffic?

Thylacine (*annoyed*) Listen here, Red Riding Hood, I'm the one asking the questions. Where are you going? No, wait! Don't answer that! Let me guess – you're going to see your granny!

Red Riding Hood I call her Gran. But how do you know where I'm going?

Thylacine My word, you do ask a lot of questions. I know all about the Red Riding Hood story. It's been around for ages, like me.

Red Riding Hood I think I should go now. I'm not supposed to talk to strangers, although you don't feel like a total stranger. Our class studied the thylacine last term.

Thylacine Did you indeed? Well, that is good news. I could so easily be forgotten – locked away in the pages of some book about Australian animals.

Red Riding Hood We also call you the Tasmanian or Tassie tiger.

Thylacine Tassie tiger! Really? I think I like being called a Tassie tiger. It sounds very fierce.

Red Riding Hood Well, you're not a tiger, of course. And you're not just from Tasmania. Long ago, thylacines roamed all over Australia. There are some cool rock paintings of you in northern Australia.

Thylacine (*sadly*) Yes, I'm glad about those paintings. They show that we really did live on the mainland. But things got too tough for us there – the dingoes gave us such a hard time.

Red Riding Hood I know all that, Thylacine. That was part of our topic.

A police car pulls up. Police Officer Lee *gets out of the car.*

Police Officer Lee Hi there, Red Riding Hood. How are you and your dad? And who is this you're talking to?

Red Riding Hood Hello, Officer Lee. Dad and I are both well, thanks. This is Thylacine, a Tassie tiger.

Police Officer Lee A Tassie tiger? I never thought I'd see one of those. Hasn't been a sighting for a very long time. But, Red Riding Hood, should you be out with him? He looks pretty dangerous and he's probably hungry. I'll call headquarters. Perhaps someone can take him to the zoo.

THYLACINE (*growling*) Grrr! The zoo! Never! Too many thylacines have died in zoos. And how do you know I'm real, Officer? I could be one of Red Riding Hood's friends dressed up.

POLICE OFFICER LEE (*laughing*) Of course you are! How silly of me! It's an excellent costume! Had me totally fooled. Off you go then, you two. Have fun.

RED RIDING HOOD, on her scooter, and THYLACINE continue on down the street. THYLACINE looks back and winks at the audience.

Act 3

Dogs, cats and tigers!

Scene

On the footpath near an old house, where an Elderly Man *is behind the fence.*

Narrator Red Riding Hood rides along the footpath with Thylacine trotting beside her. Along the way they see an elderly man in his garden, and they stop to chat with him.

Elderly Man (*smiling*) Nice dog! What breed is it?

Red Riding Hood He's a Tassie tiger.

Elderly Man Never heard of that breed. I must say, his stripes are most unusual. A tiger, you say? And fancy that, I called him a dog. Yes, now I can see it. He's got stripes like a tabby cat.

Thylacine (*growling*) Grrr! I'm no cat! I'm a marsupial!

Elderly Man (*in a shaky voice*) Goodness me! I know I haven't been well lately, but now I'm hearing animals speak. I'd better go and lie down.

The ELDERLY MAN walks off stage. RED RIDING HOOD and THYLACINE continue on along the footpath and stop outside a shop.

RED RIDING HOOD Wait here a minute. I'm just going in to buy some bubble gum. Do you want some?

THYLACINE Bubble gum! No, thank you! It'll ruin my teeth. But I'll come in, too. Maybe they sell steak, or even sausages. I'm starting to get hungry.

THYLACINE steps through the doorway and the SHOP OWNER comes rushing towards him.

Shop Owner Shoo! No dogs allowed!

Red Riding Hood But he's not a dog. He's a…

Shop Owner Now, don't argue with me, young lady. He looks like a dog to me. Are you going to tell me he's a cat? Cats aren't allowed either.

Thylacine (*cringing*) Cat! There it is again! It's the stripes. I'll have to get rid of them. And I'm sick of this yellowish-brown coat of mine. I could pop in to the hairdresser for a new look.

Red Riding Hood (*leaving the shop*) Sorry, I know animals aren't allowed in the shop. Come on, Thylacine. Let's go. I don't need the gum anyway. You're right. Gum's bad for our teeth.

Red Riding Hood and Thylacine walk past the park, where three teenagers are gathered.

Teenagers (*calling together*) Wow! Hey! Strange dog!

Teenager 1 I've never seen a dog like that before. What's wrong with his tail?

Red Riding Hood Nothing's wrong with his tail. He's a Tassie tiger, not a dog, and Tassie tigers have stiff tails.

Teenager 2 Go on! You're kidding. A Tassie tiger? I don't think so!

Teenager 3 (*reaching down to pat Thylacine*) Come on, Tassie dog … come here. Good dog.

Thylacine (*stepping towards the teenagers*) Grrr!

Teenagers (*together*) Yow! Back off, dog! (*to Red Riding Hood*) You should have him on a leash. We're out of here!

Thylacine Well, I didn't like *them* very much. Teenagers, blah! What do they know? Ah, here's the shortcut to your gran's house. We can cut through the bush.

Red Riding Hood (*worriedly*) But I'm not allowed to go through the bush. Dad says I have to go around the long way, on the footpath. And how do you know where my gran lives, anyway?

Thylacine (*charmingly*) Oh, come on, Red Riding Hood. Stop fussing. I'll look after you. Trust me. I can't wag my tail to show you how kind and friendly I am, but I can smile. I have a wonderful smile.

Narrator Then, he opened his jaws very, very wide, as a thylacine can do. And he showed all of his forty-six teeth.

Narrator And before Red Riding Hood could say anything more, Thylacine led the way onto the bush track.

Act 4

In the bush

SCENE

On the bush track to Gran's house

Narrator Red Riding Hood and Thylacine head off down the narrow bush track. The treetops reach over them, making gloomy shadows.

Red Riding Hood (*looking nervously at Thylacine*) Let's hurry, Thylacine. I want to get to Gran's place. I don't like it here in the bush. It's kind of spooky.

Thylacine Oh, there you go, fussing again. You're in such a hurry. Listen to the birds. Put that scooter down for a minute and sit with me. Is that a grey currawong? P'rink, clink, cling. I can hear it tearing off bark, looking for insects. Oh, I *am* hungry!

Red Riding Hood (*nervously*) You seem to know a lot about birds, Thylacine. But I don't want to sit here anymore.

Thylacine Wait a minute. What's that terrible noise?

Red Riding Hood It's a chainsaw. The loggers are just over the hill.

Thylacine So they're still cutting down the trees!

Red Riding Hood They're not cutting down bush like this, Thylacine. Haven't you heard of sustainability? Nowadays we grow pine trees for timber. And after they are cut, we plant new ones.

Thylacine Let's get going. I don't like woodcutters, even if they are called loggers now. And my stomach is rumbling…

Red Riding Hood Maybe we should go back now.

Thylacine (*impatiently*) I don't think so. Come on now, hurry up!

Act 5

You look delicious!

SCENE

At Gran's house in the bush

NARRATOR So Red Riding Hood and Thylacine continue on until they come to Gran's house.

THYLACINE (*licking his lips*) I'm ravenous now! And where is this gran of yours? I'm so looking forward to eating her.

RED RIDING HOOD Eating her!

Thylacine (*quickly*) No, no! I said *meeting* her!

Red Riding Hood Well, you won't meet her because she's not here. She's a doctor and she's still at work. I'm leaving the vegies on her porch.

Thylacine Your gran's not here! Oh dear. So what's in the backpack, then? Some goodies to snack on? Some rodents? Or wallabies, or possums, or wombats?

Red Riding Hood No. Just vegetables. See?

Thylacine Ahhh, yuck! No meaty treats. No gran. This is definitely not going to plan!

Red Riding Hood (*crossly*) Aha! You thought you'd try to trick me, didn't you? You expected my gran to be old and tired, and nearly blind. And you were going to pretend to be me. Well, let me tell you – my gran is fit and strong. She runs marathons! And there's nothing wrong with her eyesight!

Thylacine Well, I did think…

Red Riding Hood (*furious*) You planned to gobble Gran up! Then get into her bed and pretend to be her. Didn't you? You planned to ask me to come closer until I could smell your stinky breath!

Thylacine (*guiltily*) Yes, and you'd ask me why I had such big eyes. And why I had so many teeth. I knew you wouldn't ask me why I had such big ears, because my ears are quite small.

Red Riding Hood And then you were going to jump out of bed. And gobble me up, too!

Thylacine That's exactly what I had in mind. But I was worried about the loggers. I thought they might come racing in with their chainsaws. Woodcutters with axes are scary enough. But chainsaws sound so much scarier.

Red Riding Hood Oh, the loggers have many trees to harvest. They're too busy to stop working.

Thylacine No Gran to eat … but no loggers to come and chop me up. Mmm, Red Riding Hood, you look very delicious! Aren't you worried about me eating you, right here and now?

Red Riding Hood (*laughing*) Not at all, Thylacine. You can't eat me because you're EXTINCT! And you've been that way since the 1930s!

Suddenly, GRAN *turns into the driveway in her black sports car. And* THYLACINE *disappears offstage.*

Gran Hi there, Red Riding Hood. How wonderful to see you. I got away from work early today. Did you bring me some more vegies? Let's have some lemonade and a chat. How was your day?